ANYBODY HOME?

I0181661

In Search of the

Titus Woman

by

ROSALYN D. HICKMAN

GOD'S BOOKS IN ME

Gbooksnme.com

For your women's speaker needs, contact Rosalyn Hickman @

Gbooksnme@epbfi.com

****

Look for more books about God's High and Holy calling for women by this author

Published by 4-P Publishing Company

Chattanooga, Tennessee

Cover by MS Designs and Photography

TrinTech Printing Solutions
A Division of TrinTech Solutions LLC

Printed in the United States of America

ISBN 978-1- 941749-14-2

"From the first time I heard Rosalyn Hickman pray, I know I had found a kindred spirit. Since then, I have watched and admired her passion for Christ and her heart for teaching biblical womanhood and building strong, godly marriages. Rosalyn is a woman of great wisdom, faith, courage, and grace--a beautiful, dearly-loved sister and friend."

~ Nancy DeMoss Wolgemuth, Author; teacher and host of Revive Our Hearts

DEDICATED TO

. . . the memory of a faithful woman who truly feared the Lord and showed me the Triune God by precept and example: my mother, Annie Doris Ervin,

. . . all the husbands who gladly take full responsibility for their family's income in order for their wives to be free of employers' distractions,

. . . the husbands and wives who make children and home a priority and resist the temptation to replace their children with their own dreams,

. . . my dear friend and sister Susan Moss who encouraged me until the end to complete this book!

ACKNOWLEDGEMENTS

Ultimate thanks to *my Lord and Savior, Jesus Christ, for the inspiration that comes from His precious Word.*

Special thanks to:
My husband Gary for 40 years, November 16, 2014, and our son, Quincy for all the years of "on-the-job" training you both afforded me,

Moody Radio for shaping my thinking and inspiring me in my early years of marriage through teachers like Kaye Arthur, John McArthur, Charles Swindoll, and many others.

Three of my spiritual daughters, Frenise Mann, God looks real good on you; Kizzie Evan, one of the most teachable young women I know; and Raven Cooper, a woman after my own heart: Thanks for the years you have allowed me to mentor and pour into your lives this beautiful blueprint of the Titus Woman. Your pursuit of holiness is so refreshing.

My faithful Pastor, Eddie D. Jacks, for his commitment to the Word of God and for accepting the task of writing the forward to this, my first book.

Elder Charles Freeman a true student of scripture and our "in-house theologian", for taking the time to ensure any theological references were accurately stated.

Two wonderful editors, Dahlia Cunningham and Natalie Whalen and the world's greatest graphics designer, Michael Simmons (MS Design and Photography).

My S.W.A.T. Leader Laura Brown and all the first-round writers who took the challenge and finished the race.

PREFACE

Rosalyn Hickman is the right person to write this book. Her work reveals a lifetime of experience in the Scriptures, and in the churches. This book is an attempt to explain God's principles for a better family. In it you will find Bible truths about good family relations explained, and practical guidelines for implementing biblical principles. I encourage you to anticipate God's blessing on you and your family as you consider building your family God's way. God's promise is that those who hear and obey His Word will be blessed (Luke 11:28). So dig in and expect a blessing from God!

As you read this material open yourself to the ministry of the Holy Spirit. Ask Him for honesty, openness, insight, desire, and power to receive and do whatever He asks. Keep in mind that true prosperity and success in a biblical sense are promised to those who do what the Bible says (Joshua 1:8; Psalm 1:1-3). Don't forget that those who are united by faith to Jesus Christ are new creatures, having power to put off unbiblical patterns and put on more biblical lifestyles (II Corinthians 5:17; Ephesians 5:17-24; Philippians 2:12-13).

If this book should make you aware of areas or ways in which God wants you to change, be assured that for a Christian this is exciting. Be confident that God will help you, as you trust in Him. You must work, but you must work by faith. Depend wholly on God to enable you to do what pleases Him. Be aware that what pleases God will ultimately please you. God is able and willing to help you.

It's time for Christians to reiterate the divine pattern. Our marriages and families should demonstrate a way of living that is rewarding, meaningful, and fulfilling. That divine pattern should be evident to the world as it looks at Christian marriages and families. Unfortunately, the world's problem of divorce has also become a problem of the church. But God has the divine standard that can make marriage and the family what they ought to be. This book is a blessing to the church.

Eddie Darryl Jacks, Pastor
Resurrected Baptist Church

Contents

Introduction

Introduction

"Anybody Home?"

"In Seach of the Titus Woman?"

Targeted audience:

- The body of Christ
- The "older" woman
- The "younger" woman aspiring to marry and have children
- The wife with pre-school children
- The husband and wife planning to have children
- The stay-at-home mom

"Anybody Home?" takes it's subtitle *"In Search of the Titus Woman?"* from Titus 2:3-5 with a special focus on: "**. . . Love their children**" and "**. . . Keepers at home**". Also congruent to this subtitle, is "**. . . love your husbands**" and "**. . . obey your own husbands**". However, as you read, you will notice that I have not included the responsibility of the woman to her husband in this conversation. It is not an oversight but a conscious decision. I want to give ample time to what I believe to be an underlying issue to this entire subject of women in the workplace. So, please don't mistake the absence of that conversation to mean it has no relevance to *"Anybody Home?"* Quite the contrary!

With that understanding, the Titus Woman, as discussed in this book, is the wife who understands among other things, the importance of not sending her children primarily to day care centers, after-school programs, or, being "home alone". She will, however, seek to re-prioritize her goals to stay home with her children, to teach them the ways of God, and to keep her home as instructed in Titus, chapter 2:4-5.

A "Titus Woman" understands the value and the positive influence of her God-design and the responsibilities that accompany that design. She is proud to be called a "stay-at-home" mom and does not mind a delay in pursuing her professional career outside the home until a more appropriate time. She is fulfilled in keeping the home and enjoys her children who one day will rise up and call her blessed (Proverbs 31:28).

It is important to keep in mind as you read this book that this author has much respect and praise for the wonderful moms and other guardians who have successfully raised their children while working eight to ten and sometimes twelve hours a day outside the home. No doubt they have experienced the strength that causes us to do all things through Christ who promises to strengthen us and never leave or forsake us. As well, we know that at the throne of God, we can always find grace and mercy in the time of need. So, whether a mom worked exclusively in the home or outside the home, we have much appreciation for those who did their very best to raise their children according to biblical instructions.

It is also important to remember as you read this book that some moms choose to stay home for biblical reasons and some may stay home for other reasons. Whether a mother is at home for biblical reasons or otherwise, *"Anybody Home?"* is in no way purporting or implying that mothers who stay home exclusively to raise their children are guaranteed to have "model" children. On the contrary, children raised by "stay-at-home" moms are no better than children or homes of moms who work outside the home! However, in many ways, their children and homes are more than likely *better off!*

One can certainly argue with confidence that raising children without outside mandates invoked by employers will certainly give way to the time needed to instill biblical principals into our little ones. As well, making our children and our home-life our first priority is an essential element needed to raise Godly children. So, if children are *better off,* then certainly society will be *better off!*

In conclusion, the goal of this book is to encourage those mothers and fathers who are financially able, to first seek God through scriptures and trust Him for the wife to stay home with the children and keep the home for as long as she can. What a joy for mothers to be there for their children through their formative and impressionable years and all the way through high school, when possible.

At this point, you might want to take just a few minutes and list (with the Bible open) some advantages of being a full-time mom and a "keeper at home" versus a career woman working outside the home. (Title your list "Introdutory Comparisons").

On a second sheet, write the heading "Until I Come Home," then list any ideas you may have of ways to focus your non-working hours on as many of the advantages you listed on your first sheet. In other words, what can you change now to begin to focus more on keeping the home and raising your children in the fear and admonition of the Lord? How can you make your children a priority after work?

Finally, consider any subsequent pregnancies in advance and brainstorm around how you might minimize the economical impact of staying home with multiple children. You might want to suspend your career and/or your college plans and replace them with your children and your home. The truth of the matter is that the parents "responsibility begins before conception."

Note to reader: Although "Anybody Home?" is not a workbook, there will be opportunities for note taking and answering a few thought-provoking questions. You may want to keep a pen and extra paper handy.

God's Will

CHAPTER 1
WHO'S RESPONSIBLE?
(God's Will)

As stated in my *Introduction*, I've always believed that a parents' responsibility should begin before conception. Therefore, when a couple decides to bring children into their lives, according to the scripture, it is their personal responsibility to raise their children in the fear and admonition of the Lord. For the believer who desires to raise their child(ren) God's way, it will require dedication and giving ourselves whole-heartedly to the work. Giving ourselves wholeheartedly is sometimes the last thing most humans want to do. Even with our heavenly Father, it seems easier to give him our money, our gifts, and yes, even our routine services, but certainly not ourselves! Nevertheless, Titus admonishes women to love their children *(which in this book is used interchangeably with raising our children)* and to be "...keepers at home." But if nobody's home then, who's raising our children and who's keeping the home? *(We will explore a few answers to that question later in this book.)*

Notice how both of these God-given responsibilities compliment the other? The wife's role of raising the children has a natural and noticeable relationship with keeping the home because homes are comprised of parents and children. In fact, one might argue that a home without people (whether it be a single head-of-household or a two-parent household) is really not a home at all, but a mere house. It is the people who live in, and keep the home, who bring identity to the house. For example, it is not uncommon to say: *"Let's go over to the "Hickmans."* Here we understand that *"the Hickmans"* gives the house its identity and makes the house a home. On the other hand, if a house is empty or for sale or rent, it is not uncommon to say: *"let's go house hunting" or "let's go look at houses."* Even churches and businesses are identified by their congregations and people who run them. So, I reiterate, it's just natural to connect the home to the people who live in them.

It was not an accident that God created the Garden of Eden and then placed Adam in it to keep it… (*Genesis 2:8- And the LORD God planted a garden eastward in Eden; and there he put the man whom he had formed.*) From Genesis to Revelation, if we pay close attention, we will see that God is a God of order and responsibility. Scripture clearly reveals and confirms how God designed families for houses and houses for families.

> *Genesis 2:5 And every plant of the field before it was in the earth, and every herb of the field before it grew: for the LORD God had not caused it to rain upon the earth, and there was not a man to till the ground.*
>
> *6 But there went up a mist from the earth, and watered the whole face of the ground.*
>
> *7 And the LORD God formed man of the dust of the ground, and breathed into his nostrils the breath of life; and man became a living soul.*
>
> *8 And the LORD God planted a garden eastward in Eden; and there he put the man whom he had formed.*

9 And out of the ground made the LORD God to grow every tree that is pleasant to the sight, and good for food; the tree of life also in the midst of the garden, and the tree of knowledge of good and evil.

It was always God's plan for Adam to have a help meet to keep the Garden. It was not an oops! moment or an afterthought when God said, *"It is not good that the man should be alone; I will make him an help meet for him."* God the Father, God the Son and God the Holy Spirit in the beginning said: *". . . Let us make man in our image, after our likeness: and let them have dominion over the fish of the sea, and over the fowl of the air, and over the cattle, and over all the earth, and over every creeping thing that creepeth upon the earth".* He intentionally created a scenario so that Adam would also realize that he was alone. Don't get it twisted. It wasn't that Adam was lonely or without company; Adam had lots of animals to enjoy and interact with, and of course, he had perfect fellowship with the triune God, his creator. Genesis 3:8.

But obviously it was important to the Creator for Adam to desire a mate that would reflect the image and likeness of God the Father, God the Son and God the Holy Spirit. As well, Adam would realize his desire for a mate could not be satisfied by animals or any other creature that he named. For Adam and Eve to reflect God's image and likeness was essential to God's ultimate plan. So, at the appointed time, God put Adam to sleep, took a bone from his side, made the woman (who Adam later named Eve) and brought her to the man. And God called it marriage! Together, Adam and Eve had the shared responsibility to bear children but each participating according to the Creator's design. In the same way, each had distinct responsibilities in keeping the garden. We know this because of scripture as well as the couple's physical makeup. Adam was given headship over Eve and ultimate responsibility over the home *(I Corinthians 11:3; Genesis 3:9)*. Eve was uniquely and intentionally fashioned to help Adam to carry out God's order for the home (Genesis 2:15-18). One might say, Adam provided oversight, direction and provision for the home (as Christ does the Church) and Eve implemented, maintained and managed those provisions within the household (as the Church does). She was the primary keeper of the home and the primary nurturer of the children. *(I Timothy 5:8, 10, 12, 14).* In these verses we see the heart of God being spoken through Paul regarding the role of the woman as wife and mother in the home.

What an undeserving and unexplainable privilege we have that God would include the role of mothers in His redemptive plan. We dare not trade such a high and holy calling for some temporary earthly accomplishment as CEO or President of the United States of America, for example. For there is no greater calling for a wife or mother outside the home than God's glorious plan of Titus 2:3-5 and I Timothy 5:4. If you have been demoted to an outside career over and above your home and your children, this would be a good time to seek God's face for the means, the opportunity, and the faith to come home! I beseech you by the mercies of God and in the name of our great God and Savior Jesus the Christ to explore all of your options. Examine your own situation and see if you find yourself under the authority of those who write your paycheck and subsequently block you from carrying out your God-ordained role in the home. The priorities of women and men have subsequently shifted from inside the home to outside the home.

Having made such a strong appeal, let me hasten to say, this: Oftentimes in life, extenuating circumstances have caused many of us to act irresponsibly and, as a result, some have no choice but to work outside the home and resort to day care centers and other options for raising our children. Let me encourage you with what I said in my *Introduction*: Go boldly to the throne of grace, that you may obtain mercy, and find grace to help in time of need. Keep in mind as you read this book that *God is able to do exceeding abundantly above all that we ask or think, according to the power that worketh in us* (Ephesians 3:20). And although we may be in these situations today, some because of our own doing and some because of what others have done to us or because of life's unexpected incidents, God is a God of second, third . . . chances. Yes, He is the God of all our dots. He can make all things new and He can get glory out of a repentant life.

But for that population of mothers who could stay home but have rationalized and reasoned away the scriptures for a more lucrative and prominent career, consider I Corinthians 3:9-21, especially 3:13. Allow the Holy Spirit to encourage you to follow King David's example in Psalm 26:1-2 and simply ask the LORD to examine you and prove you; (try your reins and your heart *Revelation 2:23*). I submit to you that now would be far better than at the judgment seat of Christ (I Corinthians 13:3). Listening, like all disciplines, requires time; but, of course, we are a people that more often abuse time rather than invest in it. I recall the expression, *"leading with our ears"* which reminded me of a wonderful class I took a few semesters ago. The class was instructed to leave the classroom and find a place on campus away from everyone else and experience 15 minutes of listening to God. After returning to the classroom, we were instructed to respond to God through an exercise called VIM.

V – VISION: *Our vision must be rooted in "what God wants to do in us"* (body, soul, mind, heart, spirit).

I -INTENTION: *What responsibility (faith) will we accept to make God's vision for us become a reality?* In what intentional ways will we actually decide to trust God? Specifically trust God with our habits, thoughts, behavior, etc.

M -MEANS: Faith without works is dead. Commit your way unto the Lord. *By what means do you intend to make God's vision a reality in your life?*

Hopefully this exercise will be helpful as you listen to what the Spirit of the Lord has to say on this subject.

Notes:

Schedules

CHAPTER 2
WHAT TIME IS IT?'
(Schedules)

"What Time Is It?" This is a question that many working parents continue to ask all day. The real question they are pondering is, "Where does the time go?" Let's look at how many hours a day or week a working wife/mother of a pre-schooler is probably spending away from home.

A regular day-shift job in America is eight hours long. Let's say it begins at 8:00 a.m. and ends at 5:00 p.m. That means a regular work-day is eight and a half to nine (8-1/2 to 9 hours) long from when you arrive at the job until you leave. Therefore, most mothers are probably up between 5:30 and 6 a.m. in order to get themselves ready for work and the children ready to drop off at the day care center. Already we can see the home will be vacant for at least 10 hours when you include the commute to and from work/day care. Notice, this schedule does not include any stops at the grocery store, restaurants, overtime hours, church/business meetings, social/civic/recreational involvement, or any other activities. But by now, according to this family, it is already 6 p.m.

Now let's take a look at what she does when she finally gets home; Ummm...

Let's assume the needs of this home are typical. Tasks include: cooking meals, feeding the baby, washing dishes, washing, folding, and putting away clothes, taking and giving baths, shampooing and caring for yours and the children's hair needs, housecleaning, helping older children with homework, receiving and entertaining any unexpected drop-by guests as well as meeting your husband's needs. Whew! (Remember this book is primarily for the married mother.) OK, so how many hours do you think are spent doing these chores per day? Let's be conservative and say approximately three to four (3-4) hours.

By now it is 10 o'clock or after and if you have a first-shift job, bedtime hours are getting pretty close, especially for the children. Practically speaking, this day is over. Maybe now you can take time to rest, relax, and watch TV for a short time

before you get into bed. Oh no! You cannot do that.
It is time to prepare for the next day. The child's
baby bag has to be cleaned and re-packed for day
care. In this bag are all the baby's needs, which
include clothing, diapers, food, toys, medicines, and
other miscellaneous items. In some cases, lunches
have to be made also. Oh yes, we cannot forget
those "unexpecteds" that every mom has to handle
that go along with everyday family life!

Let's turn the heat up a little more: For those
who are members of churches, another standing
appointment that takes the family away from the
home during the week could include mid-week
services, committee meetings, or even choir
rehearsals.

Let's say it's Wednesday. There is no time to
cook and eat at home before church starts around 6
or 7:00 p.m. So, we will just have to stop at
McDonald's and get a bite to eat. Several "combo
meals" ought to do it! After all, they are nutritious -
vegetable, meat, and bread. Oh yes, of course you
have to add something to drink. Now on this night,
the hours are really diminished. What you normally

do in three to four hours with no appointments, now has to be done in less time or get less sleep to make up the difference. Of course, the next morning you are tired from staying up so long or you may even oversleep or run late. At any rate, more demands are placed on your time and you are still expected to perform all your tasks efficiently. Are you tired yet? Are you beginning to recognize what is driving this book, *"Anybody Home?"*

Let's go further. Let's take an analytical look at this typical day in the life of a working, outside the home mom. Take a few moments and think, and then write a personal response to these questions. Slow down and review in your mind the reality of each of these question. Some may not apply so do not worry about those. This is a pretty comprehensive list and I am sure you will be able to respond to several of them. As my pastor, Eddie D. Jacks would say, "This may hurt a little bit," but please answer truthfully. God will take you where you need to go for healing.

- *What did you really do with your children today?*

- *How much time did you intentionally or accidentally spend nourishing and training your child(ren) in the way that they should go?*
- *How much time did you intentionally or accidentally spend teaching them God's values, morals, and spiritual lessons about life?*
- *How many hours did you have to just sit and observe and direct your children while they played?*
- *How much time did you have to hold your baby and stare into his/her eyes? Or did you only pick them up to feed or change them?*
- *How much time did you have to cuddle them and allow them to hear your voice, feel and enjoy your body's chemistry, and experience a closeness with you as they did when they were in your womb? Nothing can replace a mother's touch.*
- *What were you able to observe about your toddler's disposition?*

- *What were you able to observe about their interaction with others?*
- *What were you able to observe about their willingness to obey and share?*
- *What were you able to observe about their strengths and weaknesses that may naturally be displayed during the course of a day?*
- *How much time did you spend reading and teaching them about Jesus and His Word?*
- *How much time did you spend listening to your children about things that came up in their lives today?*
- *How much quality time did you have just to care for the home outside of the "urgent" things?*
- *How much of your undivided attention did you really give them and them only?*
- *Were you able to handle the chores and responsibilities with a sense of calmness?*

- *Were you agitated over the things that you needed to do around the house?*
- *Did you wish at any time during the day that you had more hours to do all the things that you tried to do?*
- *Did you wish you could take off work without losing leave or pay?*
- *Did you let some things go around the house that you know you should have taken care of?*
- *Did you pray that no one stopped by because you were ashamed of how messy the house looked?*
- *Did you catch yourself snapping at your children?*

The previous questions were asked to emphasize your situation and provoke your thinking to what **_you_** were not able to accomplish or get done with your child(ren) and in your house in a typical day. Now let's ask some questions designed to evaluate this day from another angle: What happens in the life of your child **_at the day care center while you are at your job?_**

- *What values and morals are being taught and modeled before your child?*
- *What activities are shaping their thinking and behavior patterns?*
- *What biblical misinterpretations are being taught to your child intentionally or unintentionally?*
- *How are your child's disagreements and disputes with other children handled?*
- *What lessons do they learn in resolving conflicts?*
- *How are they disciplined?*
- *How does your child react to discipline?*
- *What kinds of temperaments are influencing your child?*
- *Is your child being exposed to some things before the appropriate time?*
- *Is your child getting one-on-one attention by the day care workers or is he/she mainly being addressed via groups?*
- *If your child receives one-on-one-time during the day, how much time is it?*

- *What do the day care workers believe about God, the Bible, or Christians?*
- *Do they pray with your child?*
- *Are they allowed to pray with your child?*
- *To what "god" do they pray?*
- *What Bible do they use?*
- *Do they really like your child?*
- *Does your child agitate them?*
- *What do they do when your child agitates them?*
- *Do they use many kinds of Bibles?*
- *How much is really told to you about your child's day and how much is not told? And finally,*
- *How much can you really believe what is told to you about your child?*

I am sure you will agree that these are some very important questions in light of today's culture.

Now that you have had some time to ponder these questions, how do you feel? Is there anything that you would like to do about your situation or even can do about your situation? Remember in the *Introduction*, we mentioned making a list on your sheet entitled *"Until I Come Home"* of the things you could do with your time in your non-working hours. Look back and see if any of those things would be helpful to you right now.

Before I wrap up this chapter, I want to conclude with one more question. This is a question I asked about five college graduates a few years ago. Most of them had a master's degree or a PhD. I was invited by one of the ladies to be their speaker on their weekly Sunday night teleconference Bible study. *(How cool is that? I was certainly impressed with their practice).* I was given the priviledge to talk or teach on any topic I chose. These young ladies were in different cities and states but had managed to make it a point to stay in touch with one another and serve as "accountability sisters". Their goal seemed to me, to be a way to keep each other encouraged. They admittedly were experiencing some anxieties over their roles as wife, mother, keeper of the home, and career woman. Sound familiar? I believe all of these young ladies were in their 30s and very successful. They were working in Corporate America, married, and most had children.

Each was earning excellent salaries but was obviously not completely content.

I knew one of the women from growing up in the same church where our families were members, but I had not seen her in a while. Another one of the five present was actually a premarital counselee of my husband and mine. We had lost track of them since their wedding. Without knowing how things were going for any of them, I eventually asked the question that I had asked many women before them. As a spiritual counselor and women's teacher/mentor, this was not a new audience for me. However, I had not received a response that was quite so candid as theirs. I was told later that these beautiful, struggling, answer-seeking, young ladies stayed on the telephone until after midnight.

According to them, they knew the question was something they needed to deal with and had needed to deal with for quite some time but had managed to avoid. I opened up a conversation that they were too glad to finish long after I disconnected from the teleconference line. Even after I closed out the evening by sharing all the wisdom, biblical scriptures, practical tips and nuggets on why being home with their husbands and children would be worth praying about and discussing with their husbands, they continued on with the discussion.

It was obvious that God orchestrated that call. I am sure you are wondering what the question was. Well, it was very simple, yet probing: **"Why are you working?"** After an uncomfortable pause, the young lady I had attended the same church with, spoke. With conviction in her voice and with a sound of relief, she simply and honestly said, "We want it all. We want the career, we want the home and the husband." And yet, even as she answered I could discern the affirming sounds and nodding of the heads of the other ladies in agreement.

What I know is that this young lady spoke for many women in her position. The joy for this writer is I get to write books, speak, and mentor women like these! Although many will quickly agree about God's order, very few do anything about it. My prayer is that you, the reader, will change that.

I am honored to be used by God to promote his agenda and will do so until He calls me home or comes to get us all! I want to help those who really want to get out! By get out, I mean get out of the trap of thinking we can have it all. Or even that we should have it all.   It is unbiblical to think that God would put another assignment on a woman's plate and give it equal significance and/or value as the family. That He would allow you to be pulled into an environment that would compete with His first institution, called the family.

Unfortunately, in today's society, both parents are challenged to: 1) get all the education they can, 2) get the highest position in the company they can, 3) get all the material things they can, and 4) have as much fun as they can. Notice what's missing from this list of challenges: "To raise the best children they can". Matthew 6:33 says, "Seek ye **first** the kingdom of God and his righteousness and all these things shall be added unto you." Instead, it seems we seek first all these things, and hope the Kingdom of God will be added unto us! But who is raising the children while parents go after "things?" Maybe this would be a good place to mention again that **"ANYBODY HOME?"** is a book that targets the

Christian couple who can afford for the mother to stay home or be prepared for her to come home to keep the home and raise the chilren when they are born. (See the *Introduction* for other targeted groups).

Notes:

Careers

CHAPTER 3
DING DONG, KNOCK KNOCK
(Careers)

Ding Dong . . . (waiting for someone to answer the door)

Ding Dong . . . (still waiting)

Knock, knock, knock . . . (pause and listen for response)

Knock, knock, knock . . . (pause and listen again)

"Anybody home? Oh well, I guess nobody's here. I wonder where they are?" I stop by everyday for a visit but no one ever answers the door. Where is everyone? I am pretty sure this is the correct address: I checked the directory last week and I also verified it with the last check they wrote me.

Over the past 15 to 20 years, my husband and I have been asked to pray with many married couples who were seeking godly advice in buying their first home. We were honored to share in those joyous moments; from looking for just the right house to "closing" and finally, moving in! But after several months, the excitement of the new house had all but faded away. What was once the talk of friends and family soon became what the couple cited as their number one reason that both had to work outside the home. Now the house we prayed for seems to function more like a hotel without the maid service. They were checking in to get a little sleep and quickly preparing to check out to get to that next appointment. They were eating out as often as eating in, if not more, and hardly able to keep up the weekly household chores.

Imagine heaven's newspaper with these vacancy notices and job descriptions?

JOB OPENING: "Titus Teacher" - *Applicants must be mature and holy in behaviour. Duties include teaching the younger women to be sober, to love their husbands, to love their children, to be chaste, keepers at home, good, and obedient to their own husbands. Number of positions – Unlimited.*
JOB OPENING: "Titus Woman" - *Applicants must be sober, chaste, good, aspiring to be a mother or a mother of preschooler(s) or all of the above. Duties*

include keeping the home, obeying and loving their own husband, and loving their children. Number of positions – Unlimited.

Do these words sound familiar to you? If so, it may be because you have read Titus 2:3-4 in the New Testament of God's Holy Word. . .

> *"The aged women, likewise, that they be in behaviour as becometh holiness, not false accusers, not given to much wine, teachers of good things;*
> *That they may teach the young women to be sober, to love their husbands, to love their children, to be chaste,* ***keepers at hom****e, good, obedient to their own husbands, that the word of God be not blasphemed."*

What job has any greater reward than that of keeping your home (organizing, managing, and maintaining) and raising your children in the fear and admonition of the Lord? What better place to use your gifts and implement your own ideas than in your own home? The Lord says in so doing, the Word of God will not be blasphemed!

By now you are either looking for the address of this author to give her a piece of your mind; or you are praising the Lord because you finally discovered someone else who appreciates mothers **staying home** to raise their own children.

Either way, I am glad I have your attention and I invite you to come along as we explore the subject of mothers and wives staying at home!

The best legacy you can leave for your daughters is not:

- How to make and save lots of money
- How to get ahead in life
- How to climb the corporate ladder of success
- How to be the best at whatever you do
- How to live in the most expensive neighborhood

On the contrary, one of the greatest legacies you can leave your daughter(s) is a living blueprint of the Titus Woman *(Titus 2:3-4)*. Obviously, this blueprint conflicts with today's culture. Women today are being bombarded with the concept that we must be given the same opportunities, jobs, positions, pay, and even the same authority as men. This kind of thinking creates competition between men and women that God never intended. Unfortunately, many Christian women are buying into this world's concept despite the biblical teaching throughout God's Word concerning the woman in the home. So, for the rest of this chapter, we will take a close look at the temptations that tend to draw mothers away from learning and following this blueprint of the Titus Woman.

Taking responsibility, as discussed in the previous chapter, has to do with recognizing what is most important and placing it in its proper order. Likewise, recognizing when changes occur, appropriate adjustments must be made. With that in mind, allow me to ask this question? Why do we say that it takes two parents working outside the home to make ends meet? What is really behind that phrase, "Make ends meet"? I believe if we are honest with ourselves, we would confess that two people work because we have failed to biblically prioritize, organize and align our homes with God's Word. Somehow we have convinced ourselves that material things are more important than our children and our homelife.

One of the temptations that draws a mother away from Titus 2 is getting that next degree after high school. What do you think is the motivation behind getting that next degree? Why of course,to get a better job! Parents, friends and even church leaders seem to all push the degree agenda, so why not? Some moms ask, why shouldn't I get a "good" education that will get me a higher-paying job? After all, if I am going to work outside the home, I should make as much money as I am capable of making. On the one-hand, that statement makes a lot of sense. Why? I recall saying those very words myself once.

After one year and three months of marriage, my husband wisely decided the time had come for us to hear the sound of little feet around the house. I quickly agreed. That was February, 1976. On November 8, 1976, Quincy Pernell Hickman was born to Gary and Rosalyn Hickman at their young ages of 24 and 23. respectively. I stayed home for the then allotted six-weeks maternity leave. At the end of the six weeks, I returned to work only to turn in my two weeks notice.

During those days, new mothers had to be considered in a work-status for the insurance carriers to pay the covered maternity expenses. Therefore, it was routine for new mothers to return to work after a six weeks maternity period and work for a short period of time, and then resign. Of course, my plans were no different. As God would have it, Gary and I had responsible relatives who lived right next door and provided excellent care for Quincy during that short period that I returned to work. After the insurance carriers paid all the maternity expenses, I returned home to that new exciting responsibility of keeping the home and raising our son while my husband, who was a new Christian, was glad to work and provide for his new family.

I remember bringing Quincy home for the first time and thinking that the Lord had given us our very own son. The child we prayed for, for nine months, or there about, had arrived safe and sound.

My time at home with Quincy was great. Gary and I were young and excited about our new role as parents. It could not have been a more glorious time in our lives. Our plan for me to be home until he was school age was working perfectly. But, then something terrible happened that forced me to return to the workforce prematurely. Our home was destroyed by fire and everything we had, except the clothes we were wearing, was gone.

By now, Quincy was four years old and had not reached school age. The expenses involved in building a new house was a bit much for my husband's salary at the time. Because of the fire, we had depleted 6 years of savings and were in a tight financial situation. Our home burned on April 10, 1980. Realizing that I was very employable and my skills were extremely marketable, I could easily help pay the unexpected expenses that had come with rebuilding the house.

Out of necessity, and with much dismay, I returned to work. This time I was hired by my husband's employer, Tennessee Valley Authority (better known as TVA). This was the company of choice. During those days, most people wanted to be employed by TVA, and most people in our community were. TVA is a very large federal agency with sites spread across seven southern states. This particular site was under construction and both the office and construction personnel were paid very well. In addition, it was only a 15-minute drive from our home. Gary and I had the same work-shift and were able to ride together, which was ideal and very economical.

Then, one day I remember making the statement, "If I have to work, I might as well make as much money as I can". So, I soon enrolled in business school to complete my studies for an Associate's Degree. Nine months later, I received that degree and like clockwork, I was promoted to a higher position and was really proud of my accomplishments. The money really came in handy. We were able to get our finances aligned with our new expenditures. However, I felt we had done Quincy a disservice. My husband and I had both enrolled in the same college at the same time to work for the Associate's Degree. No child should be away from his mother and father for that long for their own personal goals.

For nine months we worked and went to school four days a week. I was ashamed and many days recalled the guilt I felt when we would pick up our son around 9 p.m. each night. Of course, it was so opposite to what I ever thought I would do or even wanted to do. Home was not the same and the increased salary was not fulfillment enough to pursue that career any longer. After discussing the situation with Gary, he agreed. In November 1982, I resigned from TVA to resume my responsibilities at home. Fortunately, because of Gary's wisdom, the new house was based on his salary alone.

By this time, Gary had finished his apprenticeship program and was now a certified Iron Worker Journeyman. He always knew, and planned around the fact that my personal priority was, and always would be, home. So, I was able to be home to enjoy the remainder of Quincy's kindergarten experience and his first year in grade school.

I shared this story so you would know that I have first-hand experience with the struggle to have the higher paying position or stay home with my son. And yes, since I had to work, why not make as much as I could? Well, although I did, it did not satisfy my God-ordained longing to be at home without an outside mandate on my time, nor did it satisfy my longing to be at home to raise my son. The reality of making all you can usually comes with a greater temptation: Making more money usually leads to buying more things! Unfortunately, children seem to respond positively to the new things we buy. This can send messages to moms that working is good for the child and may reinforce the idea of having to work to make ends meet.

However, while others are keeping your children and you are making money, the relationship is different for the mother and the child. It is not the same. God designed the family so that the children we bring into the world or the children over which we have guardianship, will experience the love of mom and dad first.

My coming home to keep the home, doing the *wife and mother thing*, was becoming more and more unusual during this era for women my age. To walk away from a potentially lucrative career and give up the opportunity to have my own money seemed somewhat strange to many. However, I do remember many older women in my life saying how admirable it was that I would stay at home instead of working outside the home. And even a few co-workers my age seemed to recognize that something about my decision was admirable but did not quite know how to express it. I noticed that TV shows and society, under the influence of the **Women's Liberation Movement**, were now saying just the opposite!

I knew I could instill in my son all those biblical values that I had learned as a child and now, as a student of the Bible, my mom instilled in me. My sister and I were blessed to have my mother stay home with us for most of her life, and as a new mother and wife, I understood how important it was for me to follow her example. Although my mother's failing health was a major factor that allowed her to be home, she nevertheless, used that time at home to teach us how to be wife, mother and homemaker, in that order. She literally taught us the Word of God and was so very excited about being saved. Whenever my mom learned something from God's Word, she would make sure we learned it too. I know now that no one else could ever or would ever do for us what my mom was able to do! She truly left me a blueprint of the Titus Woman and by the Grace of God, I will do the same.

Notes:

Day Cares

CHAPTER 4

WHO CARES?

(DAY CARE CENTERS)

QUESTION: *WHAT DOES A DAY CARE CENTER HAVE THAT YOU DON'T HAVE?*
ANSWER: *YOUR CHILD!*

Day care centers are a thriving business today. They have answered the call of supply and demand. They come in all sizes and have become a substitute home for our children. The average child moves in when he/she is approximately six weeks to six months old and will probably graduate somewhere around the age of four or five. More than likely they will go on to become a part of one of the many before-and-after-school programs. From there, if they are fortunate, they may become latchkey kids who get to go "home alone" until their parents or someone else arrives to do whatever they do at this point in the life of their child. So, who is raising our children?

In today's intellectual, moral and cultural climate, the goal seems to become one of the "rich and famous." Yes, even parents have abandoned their children for college degrees and/or accelerated career opportunities hoping to become the next overnight millionaire. Unfortunately, many mothers have become restless with their God-ordained responsibilities in the home and have taken flight. Some mothers of preschoolers may even be tempted to join forces with other women fighting for leadership roles on other fronts outside the home!

Encouraged by the waves of the feminist movements, the temptation for women to move outside the home seems to have gradually progressed from a simple desire to a heart-felt longing; from an individual preference to a global expectation; from a personal choice to an underlining obligation, and finally from a natural process to an unwritten mandate. One word comes to mind when I think about this progression: DISCONTENT! Of course, this has always been Satan's number one strategy. So, not unlike other women, Christian moms are also longing for those high-paying, respectable career jobs, and lately, those local, state and federal governing roles in politics. As well, there seems to be a rise in the number of women in the church pursuing titles and roles that reflect traces of feminism. These pursuits are reflective of an androgynous agenda that clearly rejects gender and role distinctions. Even the Evangelical Church seems to be moving in that same direction. *(That's another book for another time).*

Not all Christian mothers today embrace or accept that women are to keep the home as taught in Titus 2. In my counseling career, I've discovered that many wives were not aware of the specifics mentioned in Titus 2:4-5. Some felt that these scriptures did not apply to the modern-day, college educated mother. Others seemed to be more fascinated with ministries that come with titles like "First Lady," "Co-Pastor," "Prophetess," "Evangelist," and even "Pastor." So, naturally you ask, "How can a "keeper at home" or a "stay-at-home mom" compete with titles like these?" The home and all of the responsibilities that come with it do not seem to be as attractive to today's mothers. If they would only consider that these kinds of distractions are designed to attract the discontented mother.

If you find yourself caught up in the world's philosophies, competitiveness, and materialistic pursuits, just remember Satan's strategies and tricks are just as effective today as they were in the Garden of Eden. Satan wisely dangles before our eyes the very things he knows we are attracted to. He is quick to make God's "don'ts" more attractive than God's "dos!" He knows and manipulates our lustful desires, probably more than we are willing to admit.

As well, he dangles an affordable, clean, learning-oriented day care in the eyes of mothers who desire the best for their little ones. He is careful to craft the day care hours so that mom can easily pursue her own lucrative dreams. Remember the statement, *"We want it all?"* Well, Satan wants you to believe you can have it all.

God has carefully crafted the home in such a way that it requires personal quality time to keep the home and raise our children. Anything less will result in less for our families. Notwithstanding, as I mentioned in my *Introduction*, God is full of mercy.

Do not let Satan's distractions hinder you from training your child in the way they should go (Proverbs 22:6). Of course, one of his greatest distractions is the money versus time trade-off. It makes sense to position yourself fnancially to buy your child(ren) the things they want or to be able to enroll them in the finest academic, civic, and recreational programs. Well, I'm not so sure about that! These are no substitutes for quality time with you. Programs like these will only compete with your time and your priorities just as working outside the home does.

Bringing up a child must begin with shaping and molding the child internally in every day practical experiences. Art, civic and recreational activities are useful in training but they should not be the primary drivers of children's learning experiences. Exploring their personalities and utilizing their gifts and abilities to shape their behavior are strategies better served primarily at the parents' discretion. There is a time and place for coaches, teachers, and babysitters, but under the direction of the parents and the guidance of the Holy Spirit.

So, who is actually training your child? My husband often makes the point that values are "caught, not taught." So, once again, let's take a few moments and think about the influences your child is subjected to in just one day at the day care center.

Days become weeks, weeks become months, and months become years! Keep in mind that these are your child's formative years (Utero – five years). ASK.com cites that researchers reported that 85% of our brain development occurs during the formative years. Multiply those influences times five years. What are your thoughts about that? As a Christian mother, can you honestly say that your child is being shaped and trained in the way he/she should go as the Scriptures teach us to do. Remember while you are working, your child is under the influences of the day care center workers and the day care center environment. This may not necessarily be a bad influence or even a bad environment. I believe most parents do their homework in evaluating their day care center of choice. But hopefully, you understand there are risks involved in entrusting your child to others.

Let's go deeper. Do you sometimes find yourself trying to "un-teach" some words or behaviors that your child has picked up from the day care center? These back and forth kinds of "un-teaching" episodes are not the best teaching practices for the child and could possibly lead to instability in their understanding. Here is a partial quote taken from an internet article from Social and Emotional Development in Early Childhood (How Kids Learn to Share and Care) by Kendra Cherry at About.com/Psychology.

Helping Kids Develop Social and Emotional Skills

So how can you help your child learn how to play well with others? Social competence not only involves the ability to cooperate with peers; it also includes such things as the ability to show empathy, express feelings, and share generously. Fortunately, there are plenty of things that you can do to help your kids develop these all-important social and emotional skills.

Modelling appropriate behaviours is essential. Observation plays a vital role in how young children learn new things. If your child sees you sharing, expressing gratitude, being helpful, and sharing feelings, your child will have a good solid understanding of how to interact with other people outside the home. You can model these responses in your own household with both your child and other members of the family. Every time you say "please" or "thank you," you are demonstrating how you would like your children to behave.

Now let's switch hats. Think about what influences your child is exposed to with the time you have left in the day. Take a quick look back at the schedule we discussed in Chapter 2, *"What Time is It?"*

God wants mothers to direct our children in the pathway of righteouness. The pathway of righteousness is not an easy path, but a rewarding path. God has designed it so that we walk by faith and not by sight. Faith pleases God and will always fulfill His purposes.

This path may not be attractive to the post-modern liberated woman. In addition, the role of teaching the children and keeping the home may not line up with _**her**_ core beliefs. In fact, without a change of heart towards God's role for the mother as the primary keeper of the home, this is certainly not the path for liberated women. A righteous path that leads to life is a narrow path and there are few that find it! (Matthew 7:14).

My point is that day care centers are not the problem but, at their worst, are a misapplied substitute for at-home care. Day cares function like they are designed to function. They are not the mothers of the children but have been handed a great deal of the responsibilities that primarily belong to the mothers.

Again, it is not the intention of this author to "dis" day care centers. Neither do I believe that the Bible condemns them. As I mentioned in an earlier chapter, extenuating circumstances in life can sometimes force us to use various kinds of child-care services. I think especially of the "Single-Parent" population. In my area alone, a recent news special on day care centers quoted the number of women working away from home as 70% with 28% of them being single parents. Unfortunately, some parents would have no child care at all if it were not for day care services.

It is important to remind us that God deals with all of us wherever we are at the time. However, we are not without a word from the Lord even concerning the issue of unwed single mothers. This is another moral issue with a biblical solution that can be positively impacted by the teachings of the Titus woman. The solution begins as any other solution would begin: By obeying God's words. Here are a few: "Flee youthful lust," which means practice abstinence not safe sex; "Nevertheless, to avoid fornication, let them marry in the Lord" or another biblical message is: "What God has joined together, let not man put asunder " which translates to "just say no" to unbiblical divorce.

We understad that there are other valid reasons that lead to unwed single motherhood, i.e., victims of rape or the death of a spouse. "If her husband/wife be dead, he/she is free to marry again only in the Lord" (I Corinthians 7:39 & Romans 7:2), which means it is alright for widows or widowers to re-marry. Others may be single parents as a result of even incest or adult manipulation. Although I would love to address these single-parenting issues in detail, I must get back to this issue "...keepers at home."

A good, solid, biblically-based child-care service can also be a real blessing to the married couple as well. For instance, day care centers can be a means to allow a husband and wife to spend some much-needed quality time together. Day cares can provide a supervised place of safety in case of emergency. From time to time, children can also enjoy recreational opportunities at nearby day care centers. The point to be made is that day care centers should not become a married couple's primary and routine child-care provider when finances are not an issue in the marriage. Let's end this Chapter with a brief day care questionaire.

Ponder These Questions!

How do you feel when . .

- *your baby cries for you as you leave the day care?*

- *your toddler runs with excitement when you pick him/her up from the day care?*

- *your toddler resists your urgent voice commands like: Stop! and No-No!*

- *your toddler obeys the day care workers quicker than they obey you?*

- *your toddler learns values from others before they learn them from you?*

- *your toddler is happier at the day care than at home with you?*

- *your toddler's first words and steps happen at the day care?*

Notes:

Prepare to Teach

CHAPTER 5
TEACH? WHO ME?
(Prepare to Teach)

Developing a loving, giving, respectful, patient, understanding, and forgiving child, just to list a few, is no small feat. It certainly involves consistent teaching and modeling to produce these values in our children. This is why having the time to spend with your child(ren) is critical to their development.

Okay, let's say at this point you are convinced that you are desparately needed at home. Let's imagine you are finally home with your child(ren) and you are ready to get started in this unfamilier place. You may be deliberating about what most women coming home deliberate about: "Where do I start?"

First, with any God-given task or assignment, it is always appropriate to start on your knees, seeking God's wisdom and direction. Too often we have made verbal commitments with every intention of following through but fail to deliver. Looking back at some of those times, we discover that we failed to deliver because we failed to pray. WOW! Can Christians really forget to pray? I am sure by now you are nodding your head, "yes". "Yes" is the right answer and all of us are guilty of committing this spiritual crime. But we are not without hope because His mercies are new every morning.

Prayer is our most immediate and direct line to God. We are assured that we can come boldly to His throne of grace and find mercy, grace and help in the time of need (Hebrews 4:16). What an awesome invitation! A call to enter His gates with thanksgiving and into His courts with much praise! (Psalm 100:4). This is the place where we make our requests known, seek His grace and mercy, and reflect on the wonderful work of Grace that has been formed in our hearts. It is a time and place to empty ourselves, pull off and put on, (Colossians 3:8-10); lay aside weights and sins that so easily beset us (I Peter 5:7); and cast all our cares upon Him (Hebrews 12:1). This is the time we can be filled with The Holy Spirit for the task that is set before us as mothers and wives.

While I remind us that prayer is the first place to start, I must also remind us that we can expect to do battle with the enemies of God as we press our way into the presence of God. Yes, my sisters, let me remind you that God's enemies, also known as the flesh, the world, and the devil, are our enemies also. These three enemies are bound and determined to keep us from experiencing the presence of the Lord in the ways we mentioned earlier. But keep in mind also that greater is He that is in us than He that is in the world (I John 4:4). We understand that the battle to pray is won through the power of God that is at work in us. This power is the Word of God. This leads me to a second answer to the question, *"Where do I start?"*

Second, I know you already know that God also has something He wants to say to us everyday. Our time with the Lord is really incomplete if we do not take the time to listen to what God has to say to us. Would you agree that it would be a very strange conversation if we did all the talking to God and never paused to listen to what He had to say to us? So, we open our Bible and maybe a devotional book and have our Bible study or quiet time. Whether you use the Daily Bread, your Sunday School book, or your own systematic study of the Word of God alone, we are now ready to hear from God. This is not a time to doubt your abilities to understand the Bible but a time to trust that as we commit ourselves to His word, the Master knows how to give us direction for the day. Think of it as the precious means God has ordained to clearly communicate His ongoing will in our life. In our prayers, we seek; in our Bible study, we find; in our prayers, we ask; in our Bible study, we receive; in our prayers, we knock; in our Bible study, the door is open.

In keeping with our subtitle, *"In Search Of the Titus Woman,"* Titus 2 would be a great Bible study for the new stay-at-home mom to begin with. The message that Paul instructs Titus to preach to the older women was not just for the women in Titus' day, but is very much for women today. Not unlike any other scripture, Titus 2:3-4 "... is profitable for teaching, for reproof, for correction and for training."

To ensure that we are doing our part to raise up a generation, who knows, who believes and who trusts in God, *"Anybody Home?"* specifically challenges Christian women to begin to take a more active role and strong position in raising their child(ren). This author is convinced that we can make a significant difference in our world by embracing and practicing the basic teachings of Titus 2:4-5. At the end of the day, what is most important is that mothers seek to glorify God in raising our child(ren). Not leaning to our own understanding, but, in all our ways, acknowledging Him.

Notes:

The List

CHAPTER 6
TEACH WHAT?
(THE LIST)

God has not only called mothers in Titus 2 to teach our children, but he has graciously provided the curriculum for us to teach them. On many occasions, I have compared this beautiful text of scripture to II Kings 22. This text tells the story of the book of the law that was lost in the temple and later found by the high priest Hilkiah. *(II Kings 22:8 And Hilkiah the high priest said unto Shaphan the scribe, I have found the book of the law in the house of the LORD).*

This is a beautiful story that I strongly recommend that every mother should study. There are common threads about Josiah and Titus that are strikingly familiar and encouraging. As well, the idea that Titus 2 seemingly is lost in today's church makes this a great comparative study.

This passage of scripture (Titus 2;3-5) is the very blueprint that I mentioned in Chapter 3. It is not a complicated list. It is relavent to the call of women and when taught, promises to expose our children and ultimately our culture to the ways of God as He intended.

Of course this chapter is not intended to teach the list, but to discuss the value of teaching the list and some points on how mothers can incorporate these teachings. I prefer to use the text from the Old King James Version because it includes the word "sober" in the list of things to teach. For your convenience, I have outlined this list as lessons.

Lesson 1: Teach Them to be Sober

Lesson 2: Teach Them to Love their Husbands

Lesson 3: Teach Them to Love their Children

Lesson 4: Teach Them to be Discreet

Lesson 5: Teach Them to be Chaste

Lesson 6: Teach them to be Keepers at Home

Lesson 7: Teach them to be Good

Lesson 8: Teach them to Obey their Husbands

Although these eight lessons target the younger women, Lesson 1 is repeated later in Titus 2 for our boys as well. *Titus 2:6 - Young men likewise exhort to be sober minded.* The distinctive list for the younger women also gives a mother the perfect opportunity to discuss God's design and role for males and females.

Of course, Lessons 1 - 8 are not necessarily taught one at a time although they can be. But mainly these are ongoing life lessons that are taught through everyday teaching moments. These are intentional goals that are part of a mother's strategy as she interacts and engages with her child(ren) throughout the day. What a wonderful outline to use as you begin your journey as a stay-at-home-mom.

There will also be times when a more structured teaching opportunity would be strongly advised as children grow older. Family Bible studies and children's personal devotional books are wonderful ways to walk through these lessons.

Search through book stores for books your children can read with these themes included in the plots whether subtle or overt. This writer has found these lessons in many episodes of shows such as, "The Andy Griffith Show". Writers were careful to portray parents and communities teaching children that right is right and wrong is wrong. Not withstanding, the stories were sure to emphasize and demonstrate the pain and anguish that come along with doing the right thing. Oh how I pray that families would search for that type of entertainment.

Investing in these kinds of old TV shows or videos might be unpopular today; but why? The idea that these kinds of shows are "nerdy" is a common ideology that our children are exposed to and a risk parents take when leaving children with others who may not share their ideals and practices. Even in Christian circles, our children are inundated with unhealthy TV viewing. Remember my husband's favorite expression: *Values are caught not taught.* There is no reason why the values caught and the lessons taught cannot be aligned in the lives of our children. I believe Titus 2 implies that a mother's time with her children is irreplaceable and should not be abdicated to another when it is in her power to do so.

There are so many ways we can teach these Titus 2 lessons to our children. Your time at home and their time at home with you will give you all kinds of opportunities to teach. Teaching through games, cooking, cleaning house, running errands, meal times, baths, and even getting dressed, all become a reality for the stay-at-home mom. These daily routines allow her to teach her children to be sober, discreet, chaste, good and so on, without the constraints of rushing to and from work.

It is well known that children are different and their learning styles are different. Be careful that you don't use a cookie cutter system when teaching your children. God has given all of our children their very own learning styles. It is imperative that you learn how best to teach each one.

Visual teaching aids are very helpful for younger children. They love to draw and they love to draw what they are exposed to. Did you ever notice how young chidren draw pictures of you, daddy and their own image? Already they are giving you an opportunity to teach them about family and love. When Titus 2 says to teach the girls to love their children and love their husbands, they don't have to be grown to teach such a foundational lesson. When they draw pictures of family, you can insert questions that lead them to understanding your love for their daddy. You can teach them how you got married first and then they came along.

The order of Titus 2 is no mistake, I believe God intends that we make a big deal about the order of family in raising our girls (and boys). That we teach "love our husbands" first and then our children, is a valuable lesson that our culture today seems to have skipped. Marriage is an ordained order that should precede children. As well, the love (priority) for husband then for children is an ordained order designed by God. Just enough conversation to introduce the child to God's order for the home is all that's necessary. Many books on Genesis would be ideal for younger children to learn about the first family. Again, because you are home, you can use various kinds of visuals to teach your children these eight lessons. As they get older your methods may change, but by then they will have a foundation that you can build on.

As you teach through Titus 2 with your children, I'm sure there will be some questions you will have on this journey of training them in the way they should go. Don't feel threatened or alone. You don't have to be an expert. What's important is that you know where to go to get the answers that you need. There will always be questions in any life lesson. However, we are not without help.

Pray for wisdom from the Lord and continue to search the scriptures consistently as we discussed in the previous chapter. There is a beautiful passage of scripture that says it best; *James 1:5: If any of you lack wisdom, let him ask of God, that giveth to all men liberally, and upbraideth not; and it shall be given him.* Remember verse 3 of Titus 2? Don't overlook the words "older" woman. There are many who have walked this road of teaching children and keeping the home before you. Some have raised their own children and even children of others along this journey.

Don't be afraid to ask other godly mothers to share any experiences they have had that may help you with things you are facing right now with your children. Answers don't always come as quickly as we would like them to, but when we are not stressed with the cares of outside supervisors, managers and other bosses, we can always slow down and take control of our time.

Being free to take the time to research answers that are important to you and your children is another benefit to being at home. It's okay to tell your children "you don't know." That's a lesson in itself. Being honest with your children teaches them to be honest too. "Not knowing" and "not caring" are two different responses we often communicate to our children. As mothers, we want to be honest and communicate "I don't know" not "I don't care;"while at the same time, communicate our intensions of finding the answer, if an answer is to be found. Sometimes children want to know things, unfortunately, that we don't have the answers for.

For example, "How old is God? Do you remember asking that question? Well, that's one question we would do well to answer, "I don't know."

The foundation you build with your children as you teach through these eight lessons will prepare them for the world. What do I mean? Well, we have discussed staying at home and hopefully, we have been clear as to the who, the why, and the what about staying home. But there will obviously be times when children must be out of the home. It is in those times that you will be able to see the results of your labor that took place before, inside your home.

Those wonderful years for your children to play with others, work with others, and help others will all come to pass in due time. I said due time, not before time. Be careful not to sign your child(ren) up for activities too early in life. We live in a culture where mothers are more influenced by someone else developing their children than they are about their own influence. Although, it may be cute and fun to see our little ones in the limelight displaying their undeveloped talents, it is probably just another distraction in the life of the home and the child. You now have something else that takes away the quality time that God intended to be spent with your family in an environment necessary for godly teaching.

Make sure your child is not so involved that they never really experience a true childhood. Premature competitions can feed into an already improper understanding of self and others. We are all born depraved and selfishness is one of those behavors that is linked to our depravity. Premature competition could possibly accentuate selfish behavior and/or unhealthy pridefulness. On the subject of premature competition, my son, Quincy (the father of a nine- and two-year-old) writes:

> *"Furthermore, we know that appropriate order is inherent to good teaching. In principle, that applies to the importance of when we teach what we teach. Now I ask, as parents, what message do we send to our children when we enroll and especially pay for them to play, say, football, before they can read?*

My belief and most importantly is that there is a certain level of development, especially mental (development), that needs to occur in each young child before any prudent parent decides to put his or her child in an organized sports league."

In a world where winning seems to be more prevalent than it was years ago, mothers would be advised to think critically before signing your children up for such activities prematurely. Also, consider the economic impact on your budget as well as your already strained schedule.

Teaching these eight lessons requires a focus that should not be interrupted by practices set by coaches of various extra curriculum. There will be plenty of time for competition. How about after they have learned to read, write, demonstrate good manners at home, practice time management including getting appropriate rest. Home training is a good idea. Slow down and take advantage of being a stay-at-home mom as often as you can. Don't create unnecessary stressors. Life will bring you all the stress you can handle in time.

Children do grow up and they will indeed move on. The question is, what kind of children are we turning out into society? What returns can the world expect from your children? Well, just look around. How would you describe the young people of today? Are young people today generally spoken of as good, chaste, discreet, sober-minded? I know some of you are probably saying to yourself that all children are not going to hell and all children are not bad. And you are right. Praise God, all are not going to hell and certainly all are not bad, but far too many are! When we see criminal statistics being kept on children, we have to consider that God's plan for the home is not being followed. I once heard someone say that there are no bad children, just bad parents. Of course, that statement is not one hundred percent true, but there is a point to be made. Often children are being blamed for things that are the result of poor parenting or no parenting. I believe failing to teach our children these lessons has been a contriubting factor in many acts of crime.

Matthew 5:13 says, "Ye are the salt of the earth..." One of the qualities of salt is its ability to preserve. God has given us the awesome responsibility of preserving our children through teaching them to be chaste, discreet, and good. Christian mothers, how are we doing?

Most children are not experiencing true childhood while growing up. Technology along with the various forms of media have become substitutes for what were once "outside, in-the-yard, play times." Is this what we are working to buy for our children? Could acquiring modern-day technology be the reason why parents say it takes two people working to make it? What benefits did we trade off when our children stopped playing outside in the yard with parental supervision just inside the window. I wonder what the world would look like today if children still played in the yards of homes? Of course, we would agree that it would not be perfect; but would our children be victims of sex trafficking, pedophiles, teenage pregnacies, or gang violence? Where's the salt in the home?

Matthew 5:16 says, "Let your light so shine before men, that they may see your good works, and glorify the Father which is in heaven." In other words, can those who are labeled "bad children" be influenced by the light of their mothers? Influenced to practice good and not evil? Would there be such a brightness in our children's worlds that they would see the God of the Bible and not the god that the culture has created and twisted Him to be? Where's the light in the home?

Since mothers are the primary teachers of good things (Titus 2:3) and we have at least 18 years to do so, let's get started! Time management experts say habits are broken or formed in 21 days; imagine 18 years of teaching "The List" and hands-on training without interruptions by employers. Yes, of course there are trade offs, but raising children and keeping the home are priceless. Proverbs 31:1 says it like this: Her price is far above rubies!

Notes:

Decisions

CHAPTER 7
WHERE DO I GO FROM HERE?
(Decisions)

At this point, if you have been convinced by the Holy Spirit to come home (and I pray that you have), then the short answer to this Chapter's question for you is, "home". If you have not been convinced to come home, and you have no apparent hurdles hindering you from being a full-time "keeper at home" and "stay-at-home mom," it may be helpful for you to further evaluate your viewpoint in light of more scriptures. Of course, it was not the intent of this author to do a line upon line, precept upon precept Bible study on this subject, but it would certainly make sense for you to do so.

Please continue to explore God's Word and perhaps even examine other biblically sound authors' or pastors' teachings on this subject. God has so much more to say on this subject and hopefully, *"Anybody Home?"* has created a hunger in you for knowing the will of God concerning the Titus Woman.

For those whose response is to come home, there are a few key steps to take before making that big move. Of course, I am assuming that prior to Chapter 7 much prayer has aleady gone into your decision to come home. You have worked through that *"crisis of belief"* component that Blackaby and King purport in Unit 7 of their *"Experiencing God: Knowing and Doing the Will of God"* workbook. The crisis of belief is the place where the rubber meets the road, so to speak: Faith is exercied and you move forward despite the "Jordan River" that lies in front of you. Simply because God is leading you, you follow Him. Your response reveals what you truly believe about God and will take you on into the "Land of Promise."

The key steps I mentioned earlier are what I call "transition steps". These are the practical components of coming home. Each step will instinctively organize your thoughts and actions and are set to chart a clear path home. While these transition steps will not create a perfect plan, they will however, provide a plan that you and your husband can embrace and work through together.

Just as entrepreneurs are careful to put together a business plan before launching a new company, these transition steps provide the same opportunity for mothers leaving the workforce and embarking on their new full time role at home.

Finally, these steps will expedite the preparation phase by highlighting potential problems and challenges that may lie ahead. Knowing these particulars in advance will allow both spouses ample time to discuss possible solutions without the stressors that come along with the elements of surprise.

Transition Step 1: Make a request to meet with your spouse to make sure you are both on the same page about your move home. Mention in advance that you want to share with him your approach to making the move home and invite him to sit down with you for a discussion on the matter. Bring prepared questions with you to the meeting so that you don't ramble. Be sure your questions are pointed and specific. This will eliminate answers that could be misconstrued because of male/female commuication barriers. Unlike men, women tend to concentrate on details and men are usually more concerned with the big picture and the bottom line. However, this is not the time for husbands to miss the details.

Before the meeting ends, ask your husband if he needs to discuss anything else with you that has not been discussed up to this time. Finally, share with him your desire to make your move as smooth as possible and that his input is welcome throughout the transition period. As well, offer to meet regularly with him if necessary.

Transition Step 2: Establish and confirm the new family financial plan. Understand and discuss the necessary changes needed (if any) to support a single income. Where necessary, make a list of immediate expense reductions and/or deletions from your family's current financial level with timelines assigned appropriately. In addition, clearly note any proposed modifications and alternate approaches to spending that both of you will agree to make.

Obviously one goal for writing this book (to wives who can afford to come home) was to provide adequate biblical and practical reasons to come home, but I realize I am speaking to a diverse audience of working moms; some have concluded without any concrete facts that they cannot afford to come home. Others feel certain they will not be negatively impacted at all. In either case, *Transition Step 2* will reveal the truth about a family's financial status and the constants and variables behind the numbers. Your financial plan will take on a life of its own providing you with pertinent information before, during, and after your move home.

One basic principal that governs any financial plan is: ***"spend less than you make!"*** I learned this very valuable principal years ago in a Covenant Keypers' Financial Workshop facilitated by a certified Crown Ministry Stewardship Instructor. This was just one of many principals we learned from the *Crown Financial Ministries Money Map.* I would strongly recommend that if you are serious about attaining financial freedom, take a few minutes to review the Money Map at this link. I'm sure you will find it helpful no matter what your financial status.

(https://www.crownmoneymap.org/MoneyMap/PDF/C rownSpendingPlan2.pdf).

Transition Step 3: Prepare an emergent schedule (a schedule that allows mom adequate time to adapt to being home before bringing the children home with her). Include in the emergent schedule: (1) *Time to organize the home.* Belongings may have to be rearranged to complement your daily tasks. Time management is a key component to managing stress and proper organization will help maximize steps and save time;

(2) *Time to establish a routine.* In the same way our work days outside the home have routines, workdays at home will be no different. Each day comes with unique and similar duties. Taking the time to identify those variables in advance gives you a jump on making a schedule that flows naturally and establishes stability in the home. This is where you can draw from your thoughts from ***Chapter 5*** of this book relative to your time with the Lord. After a few weeks you will probably recognize any patterns or correlations with other daily routines;

(3) *Time to evaluate and explore your physical, emotional, and mental strengths and growth areas.* Working in the home will probably introduce strengths and growth areas that you may not have recognized before. You may want to lay out the days of the week for three weeks in a simple notebook. Divide each day into three parts. Morning, afternoon and evening. Here you will simply monitor on a scale of one to ten your feelings and your energy levels throughout the day. Briefly note anything about that day that may be helpful to you later; and (4) *Time to develop a support team with other stay-at-home moms.* Plan a couple of days to find other stay-at-home moms in your community, church or family. It would be especially *cool* if there were other moms whose children are close in age. Ask if they would be interested in helping you adjust to your new role. Exchange phone numbers and discuss possible times to pray together or share recreational times out with the children.

These three transitional steps are not intended to be exhaustive, but will certainly get you off to a great start. You may think of other details (and I expect you will) that will enhance your move home; feel free to incorpoate them. The wisdom to ease into your new role will be profitable for both you and your family. Coming home is a wonderful and exciting time in the life of a family but it can also be a very tense time if things move too fast.

Notes:

Summary

SUMMARY

John MacArthur, while discussing man's attitude about that very interesting doctrine of Election, made this statement about Americans:

"We're in to freedom, we're in to making our choices, personal autonomy is a big deal to us. And so I think it's just part of the way American people think, that we ought to have the right to choose our own destiny. That's the way it should be because that's the way it is in America.

http://us.wow.com/

Answering the Key Questions about the Doctrine of Election

In my 40+ years of mentoring, teaching, and giving biblical counsel to females of all ages, I have found this same thinking to be surprisingly prevalent among confessing Christians. There are many arguments that could be made against the attitude and erroneous thinking of mothers who feel it's not their place to stay home. However, I'd rather pray that the Sovereign God would so move upon the hearts of those who would after reading this book, take the time to search the scriptures on this very serious matter.

Unfortunately, it is because of thinking like that mentioned in McArthur's above quote that we find ourselves in search of the Titus Woman. Where is she? How is she doing? Better yet, what is she doing? Is she feeling fine although she is far from home? Or is she feeling out of place? Does she feel like something or someone is missing in action? How are her children? How would you answer these questions?

Well, if and when you find the Titus Woman, would you please give her this message from the Lord?

For my thoughts are not your thoughts, neither are my ways your ways saith the LORD. For as the heavens are higher than the earth, so are my ways higher than your ways, and my thoughts than your thoughts. So shall my Word be that goeth forth out of my mouth: it shall not return unto me void, but it shall accomplish that which I please, and it shall prosper in the thing where unto I sent it. Isaiah 55:8, 9 & 11.

Hear this writer's conclusion of the matter concerning the Titus Woman: She understands the value and positive influence of her God-design and her God-ordained responsibilities. She is proud to be called a keeper at home or a "stay-at-home-mom." She does not mind a delay in pursuing her professional career outside the home until a more appropriate time. She is fulfilled in her work and enjoys her children who will one day rise up and call her blessed. She is not confused about what's important and her life will testify of the goodness and mercy of the Lord. Her ultimate aim, as it should be, is to simply obey and acknowledge God in all her ways and leave the results to Him.

Notes:

World Views
and
Modern Day
Excuses!

World Views and Modern Day Excuses!

As a nation (maybe even a world), we have moved away from truth. As in the days of the Judges, we are producing generations who know not God! This moving away from truth has, in some cases, been overt and in other cases, subtle.

I have included a few world views that are pertinent to women and unfortunately are attempting to redefine our culture. These are not quotes but ideologies that I have encountered in my conversations with women, young and old.

Space has been provided for you to respond by writing a Biblical world view in hopes that you will maintain a Godly perspective in the midst of a wicked and perverse generation. Be sure to include your scripture text.

Most of the proponents of these world views are proclaimed feminists and others who sympathize with their views.

WORLD VIEW

It's okay for children to resist gender stereotypes. They have the right to choose. If a person wants to change their birth sex, it's okay.

Your Biblical Response:

WORLD VIEW

Being pro-choice does not mean you are pro-abortion, it just means you think a woman should have the right to abort if she chooses to do so.

Your Biblical Response:

WORLD VIEW

Women should not stay home with their children if they want to do something else with their life.

Your Biblical Response:

WORLD VIEW

A fetus is not a human being; no one knows when life begins.

Your Biblical Response:

WORLD VIEW

Gays and Lesbians are homosexual at birth. They have no control over how they feel.

Your Biblical Response:

WORLD VIEW

A woman's right to do anything a man can do is the politically correct attitude to have.

Your Biblical Response:

WORLD VIEW

A woman's body belongs to her.

Your Biblical Response:

WORLD VIEW

If a man wants to be a stay-at-home dad, it's okay.

Your Biblical Response:

WORLD VIEW

Gays and Lesbians should have the right to marry one another just as heterosexuals.

Your Biblical Response:

Take a few minutes to reflect on where you think America will be 20 years from now.

Helpful Resources

"Can You Afford To Become A Stay-At-Home Mom?"
By Christine Moriarty Field (Some financial advice to
help you re-orient your values and save money)

(Excerpt): "Do you know what products
are lurking in your cabinets? Clean out
your cupboards and think of creative, tasty
dishes to make with that canned
asparagus and those garbanzo beans
before they are too old to use."

**Website:
http://www.familylife.com/articles/topics/paren
ting/essentials/mothers/can-you-afford-to-
become-a-stay-at-home-mom#.U5_5q_ldVZg**

****

"Should You Be A Stay At Home Mom?"
(By Michael Collie, from WNC Parent, May 2005)

(Excerpt): "One Salary Income. How much do you have to work with when mom stops working? Give yourselves several months to manage the reduced expenses on this reduced income so that you know you're ready for the leap."

Website:
http://www.colliefp.com/download/pdf/Should-You-Be-A-Stay-At-Home-Mom.pdf
****

Debt-Free Living: Eliminating Debt In A New Economy' by: Larry Burkett; Moody Publishers / 2010 / Paperback

****

The Value of Stay-At-Home Moms [Download]
By: Jill Savage

Focus on The Family / 2012 / Audio Download

Website: www.christianbook.com